WHAT ARE *You?*

WHAT ARE You?

ILLUSTRATED BY MARY K. BISWAS

Christine Holmes, LCSW

publish your gift

"WHAT ARE YOU?"
Copyright © 2022 Christine Holmes
All rights reserved.

Published by Publish Your Gift®
An imprint of Purposely Created Publishing Group, LLC

No part of this book may be reproduced, distributed or transmitted in any form by any means, graphic, electronic, or mechanical, including photocopy, recording, taping, or by any information storage or retrieval system, without permission in writing from the publisher, except in the case of reprints in the context of reviews, quotes, or references.

Printed in China

ISBN: 978-1-64484-530-1 (print)

ISBN: 978-1-64484-531-8 (ebook)

Special discounts are available on bulk quantity purchases by book clubs, associations and special interest groups. For details email: sales@publishyourgift.com or call (888) 949-6228.

For information log on to www.PublishYourGift.com

This book is dedicated to all the biracial Asian children out there who may have experienced the feelings I did growing up. I wrote this book to validate those emotions while also helping them embrace who they are and where they come from.

You're not Asian enough.
You're not white enough.
You're too Asian. You're too white.

My name is Julie Mei Mueller.

I am "Whasian." White AND Asian.

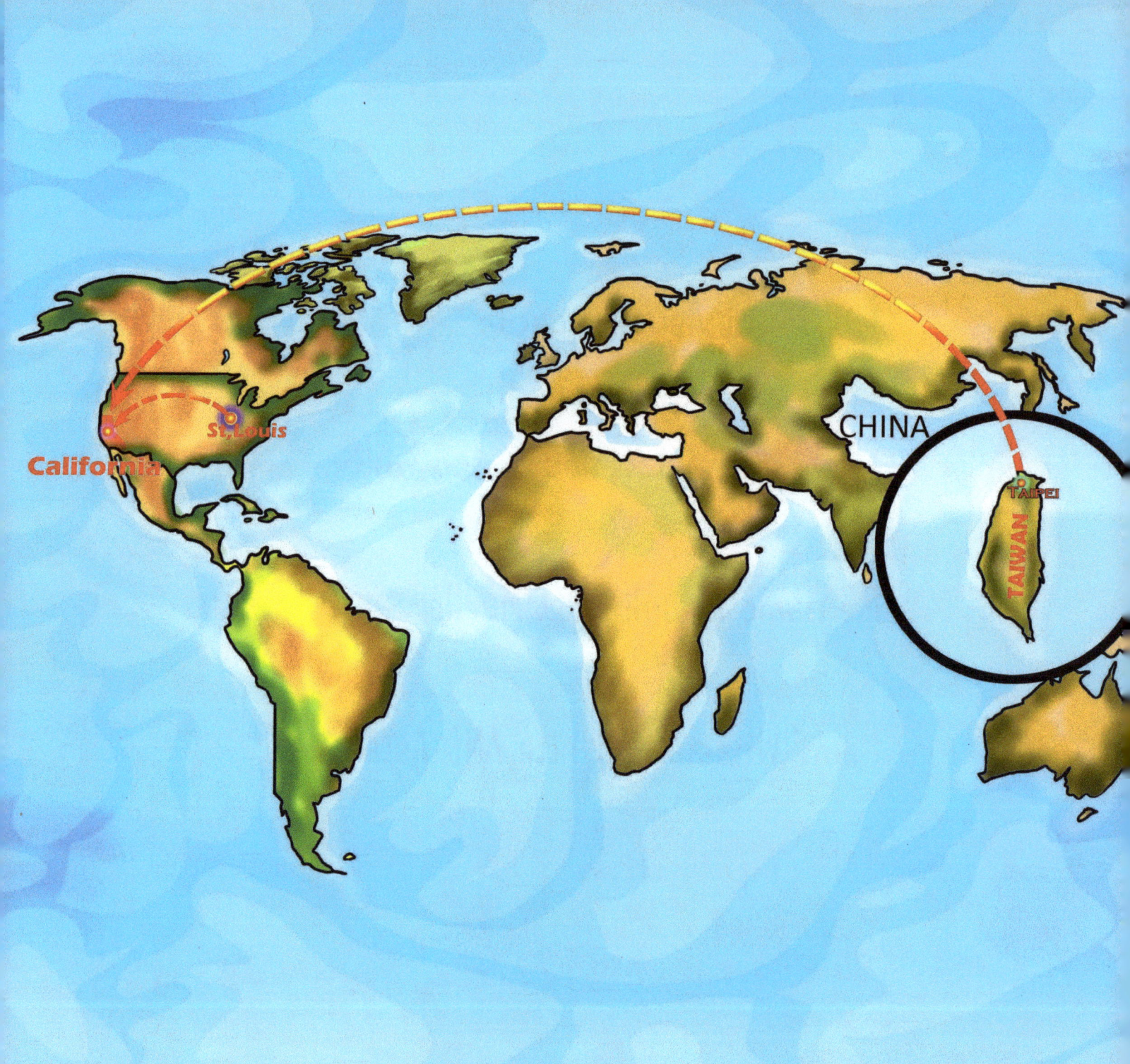

My mom is Taiwanese from Taipei, Taiwan.

She moved to America when she was thirty-two years old.

My dad is a white American from St. Louis, Missouri.

They met in California.

My mom is short in height with hooded dark eyes, dark brown straight hair, a stubby nose, full lips, and olive colored skin.

My dad is medium height with almond-shaped blue eyes, blonde balding hair, a big pointy nose, thin lips, and fair skin.

I have green eyes, straight brown hair, lips like my mom, a smile like my dad, a combination of my dad's pointy nose and my mom's stubby nose, and my eyes are almond-shaped with a slight slant.

I am the perfect mix of both of them. I am the best parts of them all mixed into one person.

When I go out with just one of them,
people stare. People ask if I am their kid.
Can't they see the resemblance?
Can't they see that I am a part of them?

If we are all together, people still stare.
However, they see that I am both of theirs.

My mom makes Taiwanese and Chinese food for almost every meal.

My favorite foods are marinated pork belly, steamed fish, green onion pancakes, peanut butter noodles, dumplings, fried rice, beef noodle soup, dim sum, and more. The list goes on.

As a matter of fact, I love Taiwanese and Chinese food.

I love American food too. My mom makes the best spaghetti, chili, ribs, and steak. I get the best of both worlds in my house.

My dad speaks to me in English along with the little bits of Mandarin that he knows.

My mom speaks to me mostly in Mandarin. Sometimes in public, I get embarrassed by it. People stare. People think we are talking about them.

Secretly though, I love that I can speak another language. Secretly, I love that people don't know what we are saying.

I speak both languages and I love that.

Sometimes, my mom packs me Taiwanese and Chinese food for lunch and people question it, make fun of it, and I blame
my mom.

I get mad at her. Why can't she just make me American food? It is more acceptable.
People won't question me so much.
People won't make fun of me.

But secretly, I love what she has packed for me because I love Taiwanese and Chinese food. However, I am too embarrassed to admit it.

My home is filled with beautiful Chinese antiques. My parents love collecting Chinese antiques and lighting Chinese incense throughout the house. They teach me to embrace my roots.

I celebrate Chinese New Year which is about a two-week celebration. I was born the year of the mouse. There are different meanings for each year.

I get a hong bao (red bag) filled with money from different family members and my parents' close friends.

During those two weeks, we have a special dinner where we eat traditional Chinese New Year foods, light firecrackers, watch the fireworks, and gather with others to countdown to a new year.

I celebrate the Fourth of July, America's birthday, in a similar way with firecrackers and watching fireworks while having a BBQ in the backyard with my family and friends.

I embrace all holidays from both of my cultures.

I visit Taiwan almost every year and I love everything about that country. I don't fit in completely. People stare at me, people ask me where I am from, people are shocked I can speak Mandarin. I love it anyways.

I love that I am a part of them.

In America, my home, people do the same thing. They stare at me when I speak Mandarin. They ask me where I am from and what I am. People are curious.
Still, I love living in America.

I love having a Caucasian father who embraces my Taiwanese background.

I love having a Taiwanese mom who teaches me about my Taiwanese roots but who is also proud to be an American.

I am Taiwanese.

I am white American.

I AM WHASIAN.

About the Author

Christine Holmes, LCSW, PPS, is a licensed clinical social worker, certified brainspotting therapist, and school psychologist. She received her bachelor of art from the University of California, Santa Barbara, a master of social work from the University of Southern California, and a master of school psychology from National University.

Raised by a Taiwanese mother from Taiwan and a white father from America, Christine grew up in Irvine, California, where the population was predominantly white and Asian. However, there were not very many biracial children during that time. This led Christine to feel different and, for a long time, wishing that she was just white. Her author journey was borne out of her desire to help biracial children embrace their identity.

Christine resides in Eastvale, California, with her husband, James; children: Deontre, Jaiden, Jada, and Caiya; and their dog, Malachi. She enjoys spending time with her family, traveling, eating good food, and hosting gatherings at their home.

Learn more at
www.compassionateheartcounselinglcsw.com

CREATING DISTINCTIVE BOOKS
WITH INTENTIONAL RESULTS

We're a collaborative group of creative masterminds with a mission to produce high-quality books to position you for monumental success in the marketplace.

Our professional team of writers, editors, designers, and marketing strategists work closely together to ensure that every detail of your book is a clear representation of the message in your writing.

Want to know more?
Write to us at info@publishyourgift.com
or call (888) 949-6228

Discover great books, exclusive offers, and more at
www.PublishYourGift.com

Connect with us on social media

@publishyourgift

CPSIA information can be obtained
at www.ICGtesting.com
Printed in the USA
LVHW080846150523
747011LV00007B/64